Introduction

Whatever grade you achieve at GCSE is a m
course, some open more doors for you thar
this book is to help you to improve your results by at least one
grade. Obviously, this is particularly important if you're a
borderline student and especially if you want to improve from a
D grade to a C.

Here's a quick reminder about what the grades mean. If you get
GCSE grades A*, A, B, C, D, E, F or G then you have passed. The
A*, A, B and C grades are the ones usually needed to continue
in further study, except for GNVQ/NVQ when lower grades may
be accepted. Often employers will look for top grades too. GCSE
grades as well as A level grades also count when applying for
University places because they indicate an all-round ability.

Grades may be described as follows:

> **A*** the grade given for exceptional performance. E.g. if the mark required for an A grade is 80%, a student gaining 90% is likely to be awarded an A*.
> **A** the highest grade for performance which is very good but is not exceptional.
> **B** awarded for good performance.
> **C** the grade which is equivalent to what used to be called an O level pass. It is often the grade looked for by future employers. It is also the grade which the Government hopes that most pupils will achieve.
> **D** the grade which a student of average ability might expect to achieve.
> **E** grade is below that of an average student.
> **F** grade is considerably below that of an average ability student.
> **G** the lowest grade which can be awarded at GCSE.

Sometimes a U, X or Y grade is awarded. A U grade is only given if the marks gained are too low for a G grade. Sometimes an X or Y is shown if part of the work is incomplete or if the candidate does not turn up for the exam. Every part of an examination must be complete for a grade to be awarded, **so it is vital that every assignment and part of coursework is completed, and that all the tests and exam papers are done**.

Levels of entry

The grades you achieve may also be affected by your level of entry. In brief, in most subjects, there are now two levels of entry, Higher and Foundation. In maths, there is also an Intermediate level which lies between Higher and Foundation.

- **Higher** covers grades A* – D
- **Foundation** covers grades C – G

In maths the levels are different. They are:
- **Higher** covers A* – C
- **Intermediate** covers B – E
- **Foundation** covers D – G

Levels of entry

Before February of Y11, your teachers will decide which level would give you the best opportunity to get the highest grade possible. If you want to study a subject to a more advanced level – perhaps A level or advanced GNVQ – you will normally need to be entered for the Higher level at GCSE. If you are on the borderline between a C and D grade, however, deciding which level to enter can be difficult. The following points need to be weighed up when you, your parents and teachers decide what's best for you:

1. If a teacher enters you for the Higher level – which contains harder questions than the other levels – and you don't quite make a grade D, you could end up with an Ungraded or U. This would be worthless to you. Students expecting to achieve grade C at Foundation level are very unlikely to achieve a C at the Higher level. This is because Foundation students will not have done all the work needed for a C at Higher level.

2. If you are entered for Foundation and your work is good enough for a grade higher than a C, you can still only get a maximum C grade.

3. Many sixth forms require a grade B or over in order for you to study a subject at A level. However, some will let you study A level with a grade C at Higher level if you can show that you will work really hard.

4. Even though you might gain a grade C at Foundation level, some sixth forms will not let you take A level in that subject because some preparation work is only on the Higher level syllabus.

I'd like to thank everyone who's made this award possible – especially my geography teacher Mr Jones...

Four general tips for improving grades

👍 **Do** start work early in the year and keep up-to-date with your coursework.

👍 **Do** draw up a revision timetable and stick to it.

👍 **Do** your homework properly, it helps you learn and understand your work, so you're ready when revision-time arrives.

👍 **Do** practise past questions as these help you to learn your work and give you a better understanding of what to expect.

What Examiners look for

After every GCSE exam, in every subject, the Chief Examiner writes a report for teachers. The reports are written to help teachers to help you. Each report details what was expected from students in each question. They also indicate where students lost marks, and points which helped to gain marks. The following are some important causes of lost marks in different subjects. When you read them, you'll see how easy it is to avoid these mistakes:

✪ **Do** read the instructions at the beginning of every exam paper. E.g. "Do question 1 and any other 3 questions" or "Do 2 questions from Section A and 2 from Section B".

✪ **Do** answer the questions set by the Examiner. E.g. you could write a superb answer about the causes of the Second World War, but you'd score no marks if the question asked for the causes of the First World War!

✪ **Do** look for command words – describe, explain, define, etc.

- ✪ **Do** show working in science and maths questions. If you show your working, you might score some of the marks, even if the answer is completely wrong.

- ✪ **Do** write legibly and in reasonable English. Examiners try their best to read poor handwriting but if they can't read it they can't award marks.

- ✪ **Do** leave a few minutes at the end to read through your answers. It's so easy to spot and correct the odd mistake by doing this.

- ✪ **Do** ensure that units are given for quantities in science questions. E.g. "A mass of 23" means nothing. Remember to give the units, in this case, "A mass of 23g".

The questions Examiners set

There are several different types and styles of question which Examiners set. These include:

› **Recalling information.** This simply means writing down what you have learned and remembered about a topic.
E.g. 5 x 5 = 25.

› **Understanding concepts.** These questions test how well you understand your work. E.g. you understand how sedimentary rocks are formed: small sea creatures die, sink to the bottom of the sea, are buried under more debris, are crushed, and after millions of years, form rock.

› **Problem solving.** These questions test how well you can use what you have learned, either to solve problems or to apply it in new situations. E.g. "Identify a rock which contains fossils, and fizzes when acid is dropped on it. It is quite soft and makes a white line when drawn on a tile". By using what you know and understand about rocks, you can identify this as likely to be chalk.

The questions Examiners set

The main style of questions are:

1. **Structured questions.** These questions often have several short – one word, sentence or short paragraph – answers in each question. Spaces are provided for your answer. Often, a number in brackets at the end of these questions tells you how many marks are awarded for that part.

2. **Free response questions.** These include essays. Before you start to write an essay it's worth spending a few minutes planning what you are going to say. THEN consider the essay questions for a few minutes. Write down a few brief notes on the following:

   › **introduction** – this tells the Examiner what the essay is about. This can be very useful if you do not finish, since it may give the Examiner some information for which marks can be awarded.

   › **headings** – these are your main points. Aim for about five headings (sometimes more, sometimes less) and plan to write a paragraph on each.

   › **key words** – these are the notes you will use when you write the essay proper. Key words will help jog your memory.

   › **evidence** – each new idea should be in a new paragraph, and you need to provide some evidence for each point you make. Use quotation marks (" ") when quoting speech, etc. and be precise.

   › **conclusion** – this is a short section used to sum up your ideas at the end.

Improving your grades in each subject

These tips from Examiners and subject teachers will help you to improve your grades.

English Language

Unlike many other subjects, it is not easy to revise all that you have learned in English Language. Here, the best way of learning is to practise by doing exercises and past questions. There are also eight basic steps you can take to prepare yourself:

1. Learn to spell

- Make a collection of the words you've spelled incorrectly in your homework or coursework.
- Practise these by looking at each one, covering it over, writing it whilst trying to 'see' it in your mind, then checking with the original.
- Read as many books as you can.

TIPS TO HELP YOU IMPROVE YOUR GRADE

Test yourself on these spellings – these words are often spelled wrongly

acceptable	accommodation	achieve
analyse	assess	believe
communicate	convenient	definite
desperate	disappoint	necessary
permanent	persuade	physical
receive	recommend	responsible
separate	success	surprise
stationary (not moving)		weird
stationery (paper, pens, etc.)		

2. Learn commonly mis-used words

There are some words which often cause confusion. They sound the same but are often spelled differently and have different meanings. Look at this list and see how the most common ones are used. Try them out for yourself. Can you think of another example for each?

Word	Meaning	Example
Whose	belongs to	The race was won by the man <u>whose</u> car was fastest.
Who's	short for "who is"	<u>Who's</u> likely to get an A*?
Two	number 2	I got <u>two</u> grade Cs!
Too	also OR extremely	I got three A grades <u>too</u>.
To	as far as OR part of the verb	Tomorrow I'm going <u>to</u> London. It is important <u>to</u> work hard and <u>to</u> play hard.
There	a place	My books are over <u>there</u>.
Their	belonging to	Those girls will do well, <u>their</u> work is excellent.
They're	short for "they are"	<u>They're</u> all getting detention for poor work.
No	negative	<u>No</u>! You cannot go to the disco.
Now	at this moment	Can I have my pocket money <u>now</u> please?
Know	understanding/ knowledge	I <u>know</u> all my times-tables.
Wear	use for clothing OR rub off/erode	I shall <u>wear</u> my skirt to the disco. Gold plate will soon <u>wear</u> away to leave dull metal underneath.
We're	short for "we are"	<u>We're</u> going to the pictures tonight.
Where	refers to a place	Can you please tell me <u>where</u> the party is being held?

Word	Meaning	Example
Piece	part of something	Could I have a _piece_ of cake please?
Peace	agreement/ending hostilities	_Peace_ has replaced war in Europe.

3. Use a wide range of appropriate vocabulary

Make sure the vocabulary you use is appropriate. Always be as precise as you can in a formal piece of writing, such as a letter. Avoid slang such as "cool". It is always worth writing as formally as you can in the exam, if you are in doubt.

Tips for improving your vocabulary

- **Do** read lots of books – reading novels can be both relaxing and useful.

- **Do** read good newspapers – these can give valuable information as well as help you learn about formal vocabulary.

- **Do** use a thesaurus or dictionary when doing coursework. Look for, and experiment with alternative words.

4. Set your work out properly

A **sentence** should contain **one main verb**. If you wish to talk about something new, start a new sentence. If you wish to join up two sentences, you will need to use commas, semi-colons or conjunctions. A **paragraph** is a section of writing about a particular topic or idea. It is likely to contain several sentences. Use a new paragraph if you wish to write about a new topic. You should indent all paragraphs in a piece of work. Indenting just means moving the first word a little to the right.
Make sure your work is neat and tidy.

5. Punctuate your work

Without punctuation, written work can sometimes have more than one meaning. It may even be meaningless. Punctuation helps to make clear what it is you want to say. E.g. "Don't! Stop what you are doing". Without punctuation, that could read "Don't stop what you are doing". The same words, but opposite meanings. Practise using the following punctuation:

> **Full stop.** This shows the end of a sentence. A sentence is not complete without it.

> **Comma.** This shows a pause in a sentence or gives words special emphasis. It may simply separate one part of a sentence from the rest. E.g. "The tall, dark and handsome man".

> **Question mark.** These are used at the end of a question instead of a full stop. E.g. "When is the test?"

> **Exclamation marks.** These are also used instead of a full stop at the end of a sentence when you want to express a point very strongly, or if it is funny or ironic. E.g. "Good luck!"

> **Semi-colon** and **colon.** Semi-colons (;) are used as a replacement for commas or to join sentences which have similar meanings. Colons (:) are used to introduce a list or to separate the main points of an argument.

> **Inverted commas.** These are also known as quotation marks (""), and are used to indicate direct speech. E.g. he said, "The test is tomorrow". This shows precisely what was said. These marks are used at the start and at the end of the speech.

> **Apostrophes.** There are two types. The **first** is used to join two short words. E.g. "It's time to go". The apostrophe in 'it's' shows that the two words 'it is' have been joined and the second 'i' missed out. Similar examples include don't (do not); haven't (have not); they're (they are). The **second** is used to show that something belongs to someone. E.g."The boy's bike was stolen". Here, the apostrophe indicates belonging to the boy, singular. In the case of "The boys' bikes were stolen", the apostrophe indicates belonging to the boys, plural.

Test yourself and explain to a friend.

6. Practise your writing as often as you can

You need to be familiar with several different styles of writing. Are you being formal, as in a formal letter? Are you writing personally, such as to a friend? Or are you writing to give information? Remember to:

❯ Read any stimulus material carefully. Use it to help you write your answer.

❯ Plan what you wish to write. A few minutes of planning can save time and increase marks.

❯ Include a range of techniques. Develop your ideas, particularly if the writing is autobiographical. If you are writing a formal letter make sure that all the conventions of formal letter-writing are followed. Here is an example:

your address and the date ⟶ 36, Orange Hill, Anywhere, AN1 3OH.

details of the person you are writing to ⟶ Mr Ivor Coat, The Mink Farm, Old Forest, OF12 2MK.

5th October 1998

name (if known) ⟶ Dear Mr Coat,

I am a member of the public who visited your farm on 28th September 1998 with a group of environmentalists who are concerned about the farming of animals for the fur trade. Before my visit, I had little knowledge of the conditions under which mink were bred, or of what happened to them when they were ready for market.

To say that I was horrified with what I saw would be an understatement. I was most concerned about the conditions under which these wild animals are kept. To be cooped up in a small cage with very little room to move must be cruel to these animals which, in their natural state, would have quite a large territory in which they could roam and hunt freely. Even though they were clearly well fed and watered, and their cages were clean, the animals which the group observed showed many signs of stress, including pacing the cage endlessly and swinging their heads from side to side.

Members of the group and I would like to visit your farm again in order to discuss the issues raised and, hopefully, to investigate ways in which the conditions under which the animals are kept might be improved. I would be very grateful if you would let me know whether or not you would be willing to let us re-visit the farm and, if so, would you please suggest a convenient date to do so.

if name is used → Yours sincerely,

signature →

print name to avoid confusion over spelling → B. Kind (Mrs)

Note the address of the sender (Mrs B. Kind) and the date immediately underneath it. Parallel and on the opposite side of the page is the address of the person to whom it is addressed (Mr Ivor Coat). Note the indented paragraphs and the ending 'Yours sincerely'. If the opening was 'Dear Sir', the ending would be 'Yours faithfully'.

The letter expresses Mrs Kind's concern and tries to persuade Mr Coat to let the group return. For high marks, the letter should be well organised, include a range of sentence structures, use new paragraphs for new topics and contain accurate spelling and punctuation.

7. Summarising

Essays are often marked on the basis of how many relevant points you make. Remember to:

> Read the passage very carefully and make sure you understand it.

> Look for the most important points but don't try to cover everything.

> Write the important points in your own words, making any deduction that you can.

> Be aware of word-limits. You could lose marks if you exceed the limit.

8. Comprehension tests (not in all syllabuses)

These test your understanding of a passage of writing, usually prose. You will be asked a number of questions which you should answer in your own words. When answering:

✪ **Do** read the questions carefully and make sure you understand them.

✪ **Do** be methodical. Identify the main points of the passage and use them to show your understanding.

✪ **Do** answer each part of the question separately, and avoid waffle.

✪ **Do** use points to show the atmosphere of the passage, if this is appropriate.

✪ **Do** be aware of questions which are open-ended. Try to provide a personal opinion.

Mathematics

The great news about maths revision is that there is a limit to the number of different types of question which can be set in the exam. The more practice you get, the more likely you are to have met the questions in your preparation time that are very similar to those which actually come up in the exam.

Assessment in maths

There are four areas of assessment:

✪ **Ma 1** – Using and applying maths – this counts for up to 20% of marks. It is assessed either by:
  ❯ teacher assessment of coursework, or
  ❯ an external examination of terminal tasks which uses coursework assessment criteria.

The following topics are assessed by 2 examination papers at each level. You are not allowed to use a calculator in the first of these papers.

✪ **Ma 2** – Number and algebra – this counts for 40% of marks.

✪ **Ma 3** – Shape, space and measure – this counts for 20% of marks.

✪ **Ma 4** – Handling data – this counts for 20% of marks.

There are three main types of question. These are:

1. Structured question

Most maths questions are of this type. These questions are often:
  ❯ about applying maths to real or imaginary situations
  ❯ increasingly more difficult from the first part of the question to the last
  ❯ designed to use answers from one part of the question in another part
  ❯ have the marks for each part in brackets at the end of that part. E.g. (3).

It is worth remembering that if you get the answer to one part of a structured question wrong and that answer has to be used in other parts of the question, you only lose the marks for the section you got wrong, provided that you use the wrong answer correctly in the rest of the question.

2. Unstructured questions

These are similar to structured questions but the structure is not provided. You have to decide how to do the question. E.g. "A rectangular garden of 10m by 7m is surrounded by a path which is 75cm wide. Calculate the area of the path".

3. Focused questions

These are often called pure maths questions. They focus on a specific part of the syllabus or may be used to test a particular skill: for instance, solving simultaneous equations.

What maths Examiners look for

ADVICE TO HELP IMPROVE YOUR GRADE

> Careful reading of the question. Obviously, if the question asks you to calculate the area of a circle and you calculate the circumference you score 0, even though your calculation may be correct. This sort of mistake crops up year after year!

> Clear evidence of working, where necessary. Some questions have marks for method. If you don't show any method (working) and only write down a wrong answer, you score 0. If you show working you can score some of the marks, even if you get the wrong answer.

> Neat and organised work. Muddled work can prevent the Examiner from seeing what you know. Remember to keep your numbers in neatly organised columns: a clear layout often helps you to work towards a correct answer, too!

Mathematics

> A secure understanding of algebra. Examiners often say that students lose marks in this part of maths, so practise lots of algebra questions. This is particularly important if you are entered for the Higher tier because there is more algebra here. Remember to take care when using brackets and minus signs in algebra. Remember a minus (−) outside a bracket changes all the signs inside the bracket. E.g. $-3(2x - 5) = -6x + 15$.

> Familiarity with formulae. Try to learn as many as you can by heart, although most are given on a formula sheet.

Learn these:

Area of a circle − πr^2
Circumference of a circle − $2\pi r$
Area of a triangle − (base × vertical height) ÷ 2

> Estimating the answer to a calculation. Ask yourself, is the answer sensible? E.g. multiplying 22 x 19. This is nearly 20 x 20 = 400, so the answer should be about 400. The answer is actually 418, so if you get an answer of, say, 318 or 4180, you can easily see that something is wrong and check it.

> A reasonable number of decimal places. This is particularly important when using a calculator. E.g. if, throughout a question, numbers have been quoted to 2 decimal places (such as 2.45) you are likely to lose marks if you give an answer such as 2.448234, which could be the answer given on your calculator screen.

> Accurate plotting and drawing of graphs. Remember to draw your graphs (in pencil) at a reasonable size on the graph paper by choosing appropriate scales. Only join up dots with straight lines on a straight graph. Other graphs should have a smooth curve.

1. Straight lines on a straight graph
2. Join dots with a smooth curve
3. Do not join dots with straight lines

Take care to:
> always use a ruler
> use maths instruments, such as set squares and protractors, in constructions
> use a sharp HB pencil
> check spellings
> only leave answers as fractions if asked to do so
> check calculations involving time
> 'round up' or 'round down' <u>only</u> if necessary in the answer, or when instructed.

The Letts GCSE Revision Notes will be very helpful to you. You can buy them through your teacher, who will order the appropriate book for you. It costs just £3. Your teacher may also have Letts GCSE Topic Tests, which are designed to help you practise GCSE questions. Ask for copies of relevant questions: they can be photocopied free of charge and will help you to improve your exam technique.

Science: Single and Dual Award

In both Higher and Foundation tiers, it is vital that you learn your work thoroughly. Here are some tips which will help you with this:

✪ **Do** go over the work you have done in lessons when you get home. This reinforces what you did today and prepares you for tomorrow's work.

✪ **Do** write out definitions, scientific laws and chemical formulae several times: repeat this until you can write them without the book.

✪ **Do** the same with drawings of apparatus, etc., until you can draw them without the book.

✪ **Do** write short notes or read work out loud to help prevent your mind wandering.

✪ **Do** make up word games or mnemonics to help you remember important points. E.g. stalactites and stalagmites – tights come down and mites go up.

✪ **Do** practise lots of questions. As in maths, there is a limit to the type of questions which Examiners can ask, so be prepared!

Investigations

During your course you will have several scientific investigations to do. You will already have done several in Year 9. You can easily improve your marks if you plan your work thoroughly. You have to write a plan for an experimental investigation anyway, so here are some pointers to improving your plan:

✪ **Do** think carefully about what the investigation is about: what does it ask you to find out?

✪ **Do** remember that investigations which involve measurements are of a higher level than those which do not.

✪ **Do** read about the investigation if possible – find out as much as you can from text books.

✪ **Do** write a few rough notes and make a list of: what measurements will have to be made; what observations are needed; what apparatus will be needed. Will a 'control' be needed and if so what will it be? What things can be changed – variables?

✪ **Do** use your notes to write down your plan carefully. Using good English, say what apparatus you will use and what measurements and observations you hope to make.

✪ **Do** your best to include a prediction. Say what you think might happen and what you hope to show by doing the experiment. Be brief and to the point.

✪ **Do** draw up a results table. Make sure that you include space for units – g, kg, cm^3, etc. Include a column for colour changes if necessary and include a column for other observations.

✪ **Do** look carefully at your results: look for patterns. Try to explain what your results show. Do they support your prediction? If not, try to explain why. Are there any odd results? Do these need to be looked at again? Is there a reason for the odd results?

✪ **Do** keep your explanations simple – don't try to be too complicated. Make sure you link results to theory. E.g. if measuring how the resistance in a wire changes as the length of wire changes, use the evidence to conclude scientifically that the resistance is directly proportional to the length of wire.

✪ **Do** make sure you use scientific language. E.g. photosynthesis, neutralisation, etc. Don't use vague language such as 'hotter' when you mean higher temperature.

✪ **Do** evaluate your work. E.g. comment or make suggestions – on experimental procedure, about anomalous results and how these could affect the outcome of the experiment, line of best fit on graphs, etc.; about adjustments which might give more accurate results, which could extend or improve the work.

Look at this example of an investigation. You might like to spend 5 minutes making a brief plan before you look at the ideas provided for a plan answer. Can you write this up in full, using good English?

✪ **Investigation:** The assignment asks you to investigate the factors which might affect the current in a circuit.

What factors could affect the current? They include: the size of the battery, the resistance of a bulb or other equipment in the circuit, the temperature, etc. The effect of changing the length of a piece of resistance wire on current flow could be a useful investigation. This gives an opportunity for you to:

❭ make a prediction
❭ test your prediction using measurements
❭ indicate your understanding of theory – and how to put it into practice
❭ record results – in tabular and graphical form
❭ make comments upon the procedure and make suggestions for further work.

✪ **Prediction:** According to Ohm's Law, at constant temperature, the voltage in a wire will be directly proportional to the current, i.e. if voltage doubles the current will double. Since the resistance in a short wire should be less than in a longer wire, more current should flow in short wires than in long wires. If the length of a piece of wire is doubled the current should be halved, provided that the type of wire, the voltage and temperature are the same.

More students pass more exams with Letts

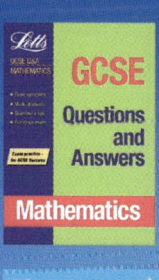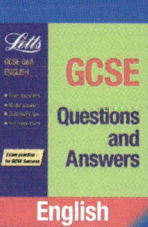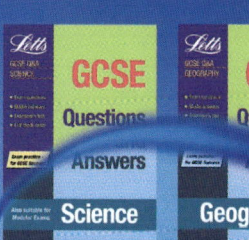

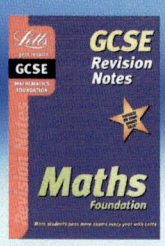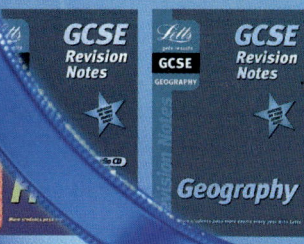

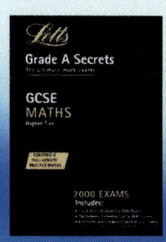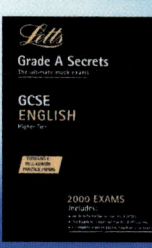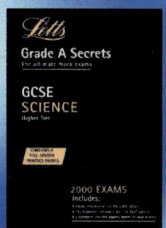

More students pass

Title	ISBN	Price	Qty	Value
REVISE GCSE (New Edition June 2001)	**• Comprehensive course companion**			
Biology	185805 9291	£9.99		
Business Studies	185805 9380	£9.99		
Chemistry	185805 9305	£9.99		
Design and Technology	185805 9399	£9.99		
English	185805 4249	£9.99		
English Literature	185805 4257	£9.99		
French (with audio CD)	185805 933X	£13.99		
Geography	185805 9364	£9.99		
German (with audio CD)	185805 9356	£13.99		
History (Modern World History)	185805 9372	£9.99		
Information Technology	185805 9402	£9.99		
Mathematics	185805 9321	£9.99		
Physical Education	185805 9410	£9.99		
Physics	185805 9313	£9.99		
Religious Studies	185805 9429	£9.99		
Science (Double award)	185805 9283	£11.99		
Spanish (with audio CD)	185805 9348	£13.99		
GCSE QUESTIONS AND ANSWERS	**• Exam practice**			
Biology	185805 6284	£5.99		
Business Studies	185805 6292	£5.99		
Chemistry	185805 6306	£5.99		
English	185805 6314	£5.99		
French (with audio CD)	185805 6322	£8.99		
Geography	185805 6330	£5.99		
German (with audio CD)	185805 6349	£8.99		
Information Technology	185805 6357	£5.99		
Mathematics	185805 6365	£5.99		
Mathematics to A*	185805 6373	£5.99		
Modern World History	185805 6381	£5.99		
Physics	185805 639X	£5.99		
Schools History Project	185805 6403	£5.99		
Science (Single & Double)	185805 6411	£7.99		
Spanish (with audio CD)	185805 642X	£8.99		

re exams with Letts

Title	ISBN	Price	Qty	Value
GCSE IN A WEEK	• **Timed revision programme**			
Biology	184805 3417	£4.99		
Business Studies	184805 3484	£4.99		
Chemistry	184805 3425	£4.99		
English	184805 3468	£4.99		
French (with audio CD)	184805 3476	£8.99		
Geography	184805 3492	£4.99		
Mathematics	184805 3441	£4.99		
Mathematics to A*	184805 345X	£4.99		
Modern World History	184805 3506	£4.99		
Physics	184805 3433	£4.99		
Science	184805 3409	£6.99		
GCSE GRADE A SECRETS	• **Exam advantage**			
Biology	185805 8309	£9.99		
Chemistry	185805 8317	£9.99		
English - Higher Tier	185805 8325	£9.99		
Maths - Higher Tier	185805 8333	£9.99		
Physics	185805 8341	£9.99		
Science - Higher Tier	185805 835X	£9.99		
GCSE Revision Notes	• **Core content summarised**			
* Ask your teacher about how to get a school price				
English	184085 4847	£3.50*		
French (contains audio CD)	184085 4820	£6.50*		
Geography	184085 4839	£3.50*		
Science Foundation (General)	184085 4693	£3.50*		
Science Foundation (NEAB)	184085 4715	£3.50*		
Science Higher (General)	184085 4707	£3.50*		
Science Higher (NEAB)	184085 4723	£3.50*		
Biology	184085 4731	£3.50*		
Chemistry	184085 474X	£3.50*		
Physics	184085 4758	£3.50*		
Mathematics Foundation (General)	184085 4766	£3.50*		
Mathematics Foundation (EDEXCEL)	184085 4790	£3.50*		
Mathematics Intermediate (General)	184085 4774	£3.50*		
Mathematics Intermediate (EDEXCEL)	184085 4804	£3.50*		
Mathematics Higher (General)	184085 4782	£3.50*		
Mathematics Higher (EDEXCEL)	184085 4812	£3.50*		
		Sub Total		
		Postage		
		Grand Total £		

# How to Order

SIMPLY FILL OUT THE FORM **USING BLOCK CAPITALS** AND RETURN IT TO LETTS EDUCATIONAL AT THE ADDRESS BELOW.

YOUR DETAILS (BLOCK CAPITALS PLEASE)

TITLE (DR/MR/MRS/MS)   INITIALS   SURNAME

ADDRESS

POSTCODE

TEL NO   FAX NO

E-MAIL

PAYMENT DETAILS

Cheque enclosed for £ _____ payable to The Book Service Ltd.

Postage & Packing; £2.50 p+p for the first book, £1.00 per book thereafter.

☐ Please charge my VISA/Mastercard/Amex/Switch/Delta   Expires   Issue No for Switch/Delta

ISBN 1-84085-586-X

Signature _____

THERE ARE 4 WAYS TO ORDER All orders should be sent direct to Letts Educational.

FAX THIS FORM TO:	POST THIS FORM TO:	PHONE US FREE ON:	E-MAIL
020 8740 2280	LETTS EDUCATIONAL, FREEPOST, ALDINE PLACE, LONDON W12 8BR	0800 216 592	mail@lettsed.co.uk

⭐ **Plan:** Set up a circuit containing battery, ammeter, resistance wire (the wire being tested), voltmeter and switch. Measure the voltage and the current flowing in the circuit for different lengths of wire – vary each length by, say, 5cm. Keep the temperature of the wire as constant as possible by pressing the switch just long enough to read the ammeter and voltmeter and record the results, not touching the wire and keeping out of draughts. Take readings for at least four different lengths of wire. Take several readings for each length and find the average. Record results in a results table and plot a graph of current against length of wire. Calculate the resistance for each length of wire using R = V/I. You could plot resistance (r) against length of wire (cm).

⭐ **Conclusion:** The results indicate that the resistance increases as the length of wire increases – the results support the prediction that the current flow is halved if the length of wire is doubled. Explain this using your knowledge that current measures the flow of electrons, that voltage measures the force which is pushing the electrons round the circuit and that the greater the resistance the more force is needed to drive the electrons round the circuit. So, if the voltage is constant, current falls as resistance increases.

⭐ **Evaluation:** Since three readings of current and voltage were taken for each length of wire, these will be quite accurate. In this experiment the resistances of the connecting wires, the ammeter, the battery and the voltmeter were all taken to be constant. Comment on this assumption – is it always correct? Did the voltage always stay constant? If not, could you use different equipment to make sure that it does? What effect will this have on your results? Explain odd results – was one result off the straight line? Could this be explained by, for example, the wire heating up? Could there be other explanations? Look at the results – could they have been improved? If so, how? E.g. Use longer pieces of wire and vary the length by, say, 10cm so that there are larger changes (the bigger the change the smaller the error). Use a larger number of measurements so that the graph is more accurate. Do a similar experiment to find out what happens if wire of larger, or smaller, diameters is used with the same length. Does this make a difference? Can you make any more suggestions?

Types of questions

Most questions in science papers are structured questions. These often require short answers. Just as in maths, if you get a wrong answer in one part which is used in another part of the question you can still score most of the marks – provided you use the wrong answer correctly! As in maths, remember:

- **Do** read the question – Examiners are not trying to trick you.
- **Do** show working in calculations.
- **Do** remember to include units. E.g. a mass of '65' is meaningless. It should be '65g' or '65kg'.
- **Do** remember that marks usually correspond to the number of points you need to make.
- **Do** be neat and use proper English.

TIPS THAT CAN HELP BOOST YOUR GRADE

Improve your science grade

- **Do** make sure you understand: area, force, gravity, mass, pressure and weight.

- ✪ **Do** practise calculations, particularly chemistry calculations which use formulae and equations.
- ✪ **Do** take care when drawing graphs.
- ✪ **Do** draw neat diagrams and label them clearly.
- ✪ **Do** answer the question asked. E.g. if a question asks you to say what change you would see when a clean iron nail is added to copper sulphate solution, the full answer is that the solution changes from blue to colourless and a pink deposit is seen on the iron. Just to say "it goes colourless" loses the mark for "blue".

Learn these essential formulae

Foundation (and Higher Tier)

Acceleration (m/s^2) = (final velocity [v] − starting velocity [u]) ÷ time [t]

$$a = \frac{(v - u)}{t}$$

Average speed (m/s) = distance travelled [s] ÷ time [t]

$$v = \frac{s}{t}$$

Electrical power (W or kW) = current[I] x voltage [V]

P = I x V

Voltage (V) = current [I] x resistance [R]

V = I x R

Pressure (N/m^2) = force ÷ area

$$P = \frac{F}{A}$$

Work done (Nm) = force x distance moved (d)

W = F x d

Higher Tier

Charge [Q] (Coulombs C) = current [I] x time (seconds)

Q = I x t

Force (N) = mass [kg] x acceleration [a]

F = m x a

$$\frac{\text{Primary voltage}}{\text{Secondary voltage}} = \frac{\text{number of primary turns}}{\text{number of secondary turns}}$$

$$\frac{V_p}{V_s} = \frac{N_p}{N_s}$$

Speed of sound = frequency (n) x wavelength (lambda – λ)

v = n x λ

(The speed of sound formula applies to the speed of any wave form.)

The Letts GCSE Revision Notes are available for your science tier – these are also priced at £3. They can be bought directly from Letts, or your teacher will buy them for you. These books will help you a lot in learning and revising your work. Your teacher may also have a CD-ROM or book on Letts GCSE Topic Tests. These contain GCSE questions and answers to help you practise questions. Ask you teacher for a copy – they are free to you.

Geography

If you are taking geography at GCSE, read on. If not jump to the next section.

Thorough learning and appropriate revision is needed, in addition to good quality coursework, in order to improve your geography grade. Once again, plenty of practice at doing exam questions is important. When you have completed a section of the work, use past exam questions to help you learn and revise it. Make sure that your case studies are thorough and well-written. Learn them if you can, as you may well be asked questions about them.

There are three main types of question. These are:

1. Multiple choice

Only a few Exam Boards still use this type of question in geography. Check with your teacher. If your syllabus uses multiple choice questions, you will be given a question followed by four possible answers labelled A, B, C and D. Only one of these answers is correct. Remember to complete the following steps for each multiple choice question:

1. Read the question.
2. Look carefully at each of the answers.
3. Choose and carefully mark the computer answer sheet at the correct point.

If you are not sure of the answer – or you don't know it – you may still be able to work it out. Look at each of the answers and cross out those which you know are wrong. If only one remains, that must be the right answer. If more than one remain, you have at least reduced the number of possibilities. Don't leave any questions unanswered. You have, at worst, 1 chance in 4 of getting it right!

2. Structured questions

As in other subjects, this will be the most common type of question. In geography many structured questions include photographs, maps, diagrams, or even articles from newspapers. It is important that you read or look carefully at all the information given: it is all there to help you. Examiners may test your understanding by asking you to apply your knowledge to new situations. E.g. you might have studied coastal pollution around the Thames estuary, but Examiners may ask you about coastal pollution at, say, the Rhine estuary. If they do, don't worry – they will provide sufficient information to enable you to answer the question.

As in most subjects, the first parts of structured questions are the easiest, but each part gets gradually more difficult so that the hardest part – which the highest-grade candidates need to get right – is at the end.

In some geography syllabuses, the last part of a question may be based on a case study that you will have made during the course. It's very important, therefore, that your coursework is of the highest standard you can manage.

Choice of questions

When choosing the questions you are going to attempt in an exam paper that has case studies, go to the end of the questions first and compare the case studies and decide which you could do best. This should help inform your choice.

3. Essay questions

These are rare in GCSE geography papers, but may occasionally be found in some Higher tier papers. As with all essay questions these need planning.

✪ **Do** jot down a list of important points.

✪ **Do** put the points in the order you wish to write about.

✪ **Do** write a new paragraph for each point.

✪ **Do** include drawings or diagrams to help explain points.

In many geography questions you will be asked to draw either sketch maps or diagrams. You should use maps and drawings to illustrate your answers. They always make answering easier and help you score more marks.

Sketch maps and drawings are vital to geographers: make sure that you draw and label them accurately. Good sketches gain marks and can help with your explanations.

What geography Examiners look for

Geography Examiners are looking for clear evidence of specific knowledge and its application, so:

✪ **Do** make sure that your case studies and field work are first class.

✪ **Do** respond to command words such as 'describe' or 'explain'.

✪ **Do** take time and care over graphical skills, e.g. when asked to read or complete a graph or map. It is easy to rush and make simple errors and lose marks.

✪ **Look** at the marks available for each question or part of a question. Use it as an indication of how much to write.

✪ **Do** make sure that you attempt every part of a question.

✪ **Do** be specific with your details: a sense of place is important, so link facts with locations.

TIPS TO HELP IMPROVE YOUR GRADE

- **Do** give comparisons if asked to describe differences. E.g. if asked to describe differences between a regional shopping centre and high street retail outlets, you need to say things like "regional centres have larger car parks" rather than "they have large car parks".

- **Do** illustrate longer answers with examples from case studies when appropriate.

- **Do** use drawings to support your answers where appropriate.

- **Do** make sure that you are fully familiar with Ordnance Survey maps and their symbols, and the skills you need to use them, e.g. using a scale, using grid references.

Letts Geography GCSE Revision notes are also available, price £3. These notes can be a lot of help in revising. Your teacher may have a copy of Letts Geography Topic Tests. These are questions and answers in geography which are free to you, so get yourself a copy of relevant questions.

History

If you have studied history read on. If not, jump to the next section.

There are many different history syllabuses but the principles of each are the same. Again, thorough learning and revision are vital: detailed knowledge of people, places, dates, events and legislation is essential. Since many history questions may require longer essay-type answers, it is important that you practise as many past exam questions as possible. Usually, three styles of question are used in history GCSE exams. They are:

1. Structured essay questions

These may each have several parts. They are often based on source material which you will need to evaluate with care. Sometimes another form of stimulus is used; for instance, a picture. It is worth using the number of marks given as a guide to how long your answer should be. If the mark is [2] your answer may only need to be a single sentence, but if it is [10], you will need to write at least a paragraph.

2. Mixed questions

Parts of these may only require one word answers. Others will need a sentence or two and some parts will require extended essays.

3. Questions based on the use of evidence

Most Exam Boards base one of the papers on a Development Study. For this there is a different topic each year, and your teacher will have been told what the topic is. This part of the history exam, in particular, tests how well you can use information from a number of different historical sources. You will be expected to use your knowledge to interpret and evaluate the given historical sources. Of course, you will also need to use your own knowledge here.

All questions on this paper are compulsory, so make sure that you:

> Plan how you will use the time fairly for these questions.
> Read the background information and sources carefully.
> Accept certain details from sources as being true. The writer's name, date written and circumstances will be accurate.
> Try to find opportunities to compare an account from one source with that of another.
> Use the sources you are advised to use in a question and quote words and sentences from them. You might also gain marks if you use other sources as well, provided that they are relevant.
> Take care with judgements: if you have said a source is reliable in one part of the question, you can't then say it is unreliable in another.
> Use <u>bias</u> to help you find out how historians viewed the past: there are bound to be differing opinions about an event. Challenge the evidence if you can: is it very one-sided? Use the bias to help you.
> Judge each source on its own merits, whether <u>primary</u> or <u>secondary</u>.

What history Examiners look for

4 TIPS TO IMPROVE YOUR GRADE

✪ **Do** use your knowledge of places, people, events, dates and legislation to support your understanding.

✪ **Do** make sure you read the instructions really carefully.

✪ **Do** make the most of the evidence. Remember that, in history, it is acceptable to be doubtful. You don't always have to come to a firm conclusion.

✪ **Do** remember that marks are gained if your essays are well written.

Let's think about how you might respond to a question about unemployment earlier this Century.

Question:
Consider the effect of unemployment upon people during the 1930s.

Mentioning that many people were unemployed – very basic information – would score just 1 mark. A more generalised explanation, for instance, saying that there was high unemployment in England and Wales, would score 2 or 3 marks. However, using knowledge to explain the answer, and including information on the effect of unemployment on the individual, life on the dole, means testing, and so linking the development of new industries, would score between 4 and 9 marks.

French

Much of this section may well be good advice for other modern foreign languages such as German or Spanish. Of course, any modern foreign language requires a great deal of learning and regular practice. If you go to France you quickly pick up some French, but it is soon forgotten if practice isn't continued on returning home. Vocabulary, verbs and their tenses, sentence construction and other grammatical aspects of language must be understood and learned if progress is to be made. To acquire language skills takes a long time, and one skill is built up on another.

The new French Exam

For the 1999 exam there are a number of important changes:

1. You can now use a French-English dictionary, but beware! You won't have time to look up many words, so don't rely on it. Practise using your dictionary.

2. In the **speaking test** you can use a dictionary during your preparation time, but not when you start the test.

3. You cannot use a dictionary during the **listening test**, but some Boards allow one to be used before the test starts – check with your teacher.

4. Most instructions are given in French. Make sure that you understand them and get a full list from your teacher.

5. Questions in the **listening** and **reading** paper will be in French – and you must answer in French. Some Boards use English – check with your teacher.

Here are some examples of instructions:
- Répondez en français – answer in French.
- Cochez la bonne case (les bonnes cases) – tick the appropriate box (boxes).
- Lisez les questions – read the questions.
- Regardez les images/dessins – look at the pictures/drawings.
- Faites correspondre – match up.
- Vous allez entendre une conversation – you are going to hear a conversation.
- Ecrivez une lettre de 200 à 250 mots – write a letter of between 200 to 250 words.

It is important to remember that to learn a language requires determination and dedication. Each of these skills is important for GCSE French.

Speaking   Listening   Reading   Writing

French

The **oral test** will test your ability to speak and to understand spoken French. It will always include a section on general conversation. To prepare for this, you need to learn the vocabulary and must be able to speak about some of the following topic areas:

> yourself and your interests
> family, friends, a teacher
> your home, your town or your country
> what you do at school
> your hopes for the future, your ambitions and career ideas
> what you do in your free time
> interesting places you have been on holiday
> what you like to buy
> your favourite foods and cooking
> the weather, especially in England
> health, illness, dealing with emergencies and going to the chemist
> going to the bank, hotels, post office, police and lost property

Whatever else you do, you will need some key vocabulary. Here is a bare minimum:

TIPS TO HELP IMPROVE YOUR GRADE

Learn these essential phrases and words

> School subjects
> **l'anglais**; **les maths**; **les sciences**; **la technologie**; **l'histoire,** etc.

> Home and abroad
> **ma maison** – my house; **au centre ville** – town centre; **au camping** – on a campsite; **Le trajet dure quatre heures** – The journey lasts 4 hours.

> Health
> **J'ai mal à la tête** – I've got a headache; **J'ai mal ici** – It hurts here; **Pouvez-vous m'aider?** – Can you help me?

> Shopping
> **les baskets** – trainers; **la jupe** – skirt; **la veste** – jacket; **c'est tout?** – is that all?

> Hobbies
> **Je joue au ping pong/hockey/football** – I play table tennis/hockey/football; **Je joue à mon ordinateur** – I play on my computer; **Je vais à la discothèque** – I go to the disco; **J'aime la natation** OR **J'aime nager** – I like swimming; **Je vais au stade pour regarder un match de football** – I go to the football ground to watch a match.

> Numbers
> **You must learn all of them.** Learn to recognise numbers both spoken and written – learn what they look like and what they sound like. Remember that the sound can change. E.g. **dix minutes** (pronounced 'dee') – ten minutes; compared with – Il est **dix** heures <u>**dix**</u> – (**dix** – pronounced 'deez'; <u>**dix**</u> pronounced 'dees').

Verbs

You must know: present; perfect; future and imperfect tenses of verbs. You also need to know and use the conditional and pluperfect tenses. Eg:

> **Present tense**
> je vais (I am going – **beware NOT je suis allant**); je n'aime pas (I don't like).

> **Future tense**
> j'aurai (I shall have) – tu seras (you will be)

> **Conditional tense**
> je voudrais (I would like OR I would like to); tu pourrais (you could); il achèterait (he would buy); je serais (I would be); Je devrais (I ought to).

> **Pluperfect tense**
> j'avais perdu (I had lost); Il était parti (he had gone).

> **Imperfect tense**
> tu étais (you were OR you used to be) – il allait (he went OR he used to go) – ils voulaient (they wanted to).

> Learn verbs which use être in the perfect and pluperfect tenses.

These verbs all relate to 'coming' and 'going'.

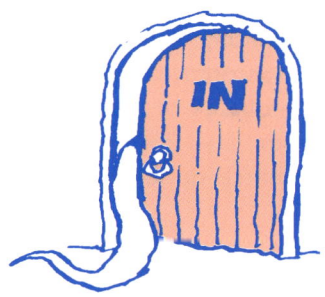

arriver (to arrive)
descendre (to go down)
venir (to come)
entrer (to go in)
naître (to be born)
tomber (to fall)

partir (to leave)
monter (to go up)
aller (to go)
sortir (to go out)
mourir (to die)
rester (to stay)

Giving an account

Giving an account, either in the speaking test or the writing test, requires preparation and planning. Write a few notes including the vocabulary you will need and the tense of the verbs. For example, you might wish to give an account of a holiday or day in your life. If it's for a speaking test, write down what you want to say: learn it, but be prepared to make changes if necessary. For writing, simply make notes on what you are going to say. Show what you know with a long, detailed and interesting answer.

Role play

Often this takes the form of buying something in a shop, booking a hotel room, ordering something in a café or restaurant, asking for the times of trains or buses or asking for information in a tourist office. Your teacher – or the Examiner – usually plays the part of the salesperson or assistant. You'll need to be able to imagine yourself in different situations.

At **Foundation level**, the information is often given in picture form and the instructions will be in English. If there is a question mark (?) by the side of a picture, that indicates that you must ask for the item(s) shown.

> **In this case, you might ask the question:**
> **Est-ce que je peux avoir un kilo de pommes? (Can I have a kilo of apples?)**

At **Higher level**, the Examiner will expect you to have a good command of French. You will need to use different tenses and to take the initiative. You may have to give an account, for example, of a journey you have made, or imagine that you are at a job interview. You will certainly be expected to take part in a lengthy discussion, so you will need to improvise and be spontaneous.

Top tip

Make a quick plan of what you might be asked about a topic during your preparation time. Then consider which tenses you will want to use in your answers. Let's say you're about to be asked about a job interview situation:

> **Questions I might be asked**
> **Tenses I want to use in my answer**
> **What experience have you had?**
> Past; "I have worked for..." (j'ai travaillé...)
> **What made you apply for this job?**
> Conditional; "I would like to work for..." (j'aimerais travailler...)
> **What interests you about this job?**
> Present; "I am interested in..." (je m'intéresse à...)
> **When could you start?**
> Conditional; "I could start on..." (je pourrais commencer...)

Marks will be given for:
> the accuracy and fluency of your French
> your accent
> your use of verbs in different tenses

> the range of vocabulary you use
> your ability to make yourself understood in a given situation
> how well you can understand and answer questions put by your teacher or Examiner.

Revise your **vocabulary** regularly to refresh your memory

Practise **reading** French throughout your course

Listen to French radio stations – what's it all about?

Examiners' hints for the listening test

✪ **Do** practise talking French to a friend – or to yourself – particularly just before the listening or speaking test.

✪ **Do** read the instructions and questions slowly and carefully.

✪ **Do** underline key words. E.g. donnez <u>trois</u> raisons (give <u>three</u> reasons).

✪ **Do** make sure that you can hear the recording clearly: tell the teacher at the start if you can't.

✪ **Do** listen carefully to each playing. You will hear the French text 2 or 3 times. Often during these subsequent playings things become clear, so keep listening.

✪ **Do** make sure that your answer shows clearly that you have understood the French. Will the Examiner know what you mean?

Examiners' hints for the reading test

You will have to answer in French. At **Foundation level**, answers are usually one word, but at **Higher level**, you will be expected to write longer answers. These need not necessarily be sentences, and the French does not have to be perfect. It does, however, have to be understandable, and show that you have understood what you have read.

Questions will include – multiple choice, true or false (vrai – faux), matching letters to statements, longer questions which need to be answered in English and questions which must be answered in French.

Examiners' hints for the writing test

Writing is the most difficult of the skills you will need.

- **Do** careful, regular revision and get plenty of practice. These are vital.
- **Do** learn how to use those irregular verbs.
- **Do** concentrate on the present, perfect, and future tenses. For Higher level don't neglect the conditional and pluperfect.
- **Do** make sure spelling is accurate.
- **Do** make sure that you are accurate in your usage of accents, etc.
- **Do** use your dictionary carefully and sparingly, to save valuable time.
- **Do** write on alternate lines. This leaves a space between your writing for you to correct errors or to make changes at the end if you need to.
- **Do** leave time to check what you have written. Now is the time to use your dictionary.
- **Do** time your writing carefully.
- **Do** use a good variety of verbs and a wide range of vocabulary.

Letts French GCSE Revision Notes are also available, price £3. These notes, and the CD which accompanies them, can be a lot of help in revising. Your teacher may have a copy of Letts French Topic Tests. These are questions and answers in French which could help you. These are free to you, so get a copy of relevant questions.

Study skills you should know

- ⊛ **Do** make sure that you get all that you can from each lesson. It makes sense to ask if you don't understand.
- ⊛ **Do** make sure you understand new concepts – if in doubt ask. Never leave something you don't understand in the hope that it will sort itself out. That won't happen!
- ⊛ **Do** discuss new ideas and concepts with a friend. Try to test your own understanding by explaining the idea or concept to someone else.
- ⊛ **Do** go over your day's work at home. You know that homework helps you to learn your class work, programs the brain and helps you understand new concepts. Don't let yourself down – do it!
- ⊛ **Do** practise doing questions. This helps to ensure that you understand your work, gives you practice in doing research, and helps your memory.
- ⊛ **Do** develop ways of memorising information. Write notes or read aloud – this helps concentration. Keep doing this until you can remember all the information easily.
- ✖ **Don't** let yourself get tired. Your brain will be 'fuzzy' after a really late night and even easy tasks may seem harder.
- ✖ **Don't** worry if you haven't solved every single problem before you finish your evening's work. The brain is a problem solver and can solve problems while you are asleep – use it!

You can improve your grades if you follow the advice from this book. It takes a lot of hard work and dedication, but it's worth it in the end: you've really achieved something.

When the exams are over, go and enjoy yourself. Don't worry: you can't change anything by worrying. The worst that can happen is that you might have to repeat a subject, or change a plan.